Wobbly Lines Art NZ

Thank you for purchasing my art. Your support means so much to me!

This Fashion Book has been a labour of love. I have been interested in fashion all my life, even though I'm not at all fashionable. But, I do like to draw women's clothing, and I enjoy putting my whimsical spin on it. Most of it is probably not everyday wearable, but I would love to see them being worn.
I think they would be a lot of fun to create.
And even more fun to wear.

You have my permission to use these designs for your own personal use for inspiration, to create your own clothes.

Due to the nature of my hand-drawn art, there will be wobbly lines that are part of the charm of non-digital art. **There are 30 A4 pages in this book. Plus 10 A5 pages, with TWO pocket-sized/Postcard sized pictures on each page**. If you want, after colouring the A5 images, cut them out and send as a postcard. If you copy them directly onto thickish card you can send them as they are. If you copy onto thin card, or paper {as I do}, just mount them onto card with double-sided tape or glue after you've finished colouring. Pop on a stamp and post!

I invite you to join and share your finished page in my Facebook Coloring Group at
www.facebook.com/groups/WobblyLines/
My Art Page on Facebook:
www.facebook.com/WobblyLines/

PLEASE NOTE

*Because this is a digital file, it is not eligible for a refund.

Thank you for respecting my art.

~Lynette~

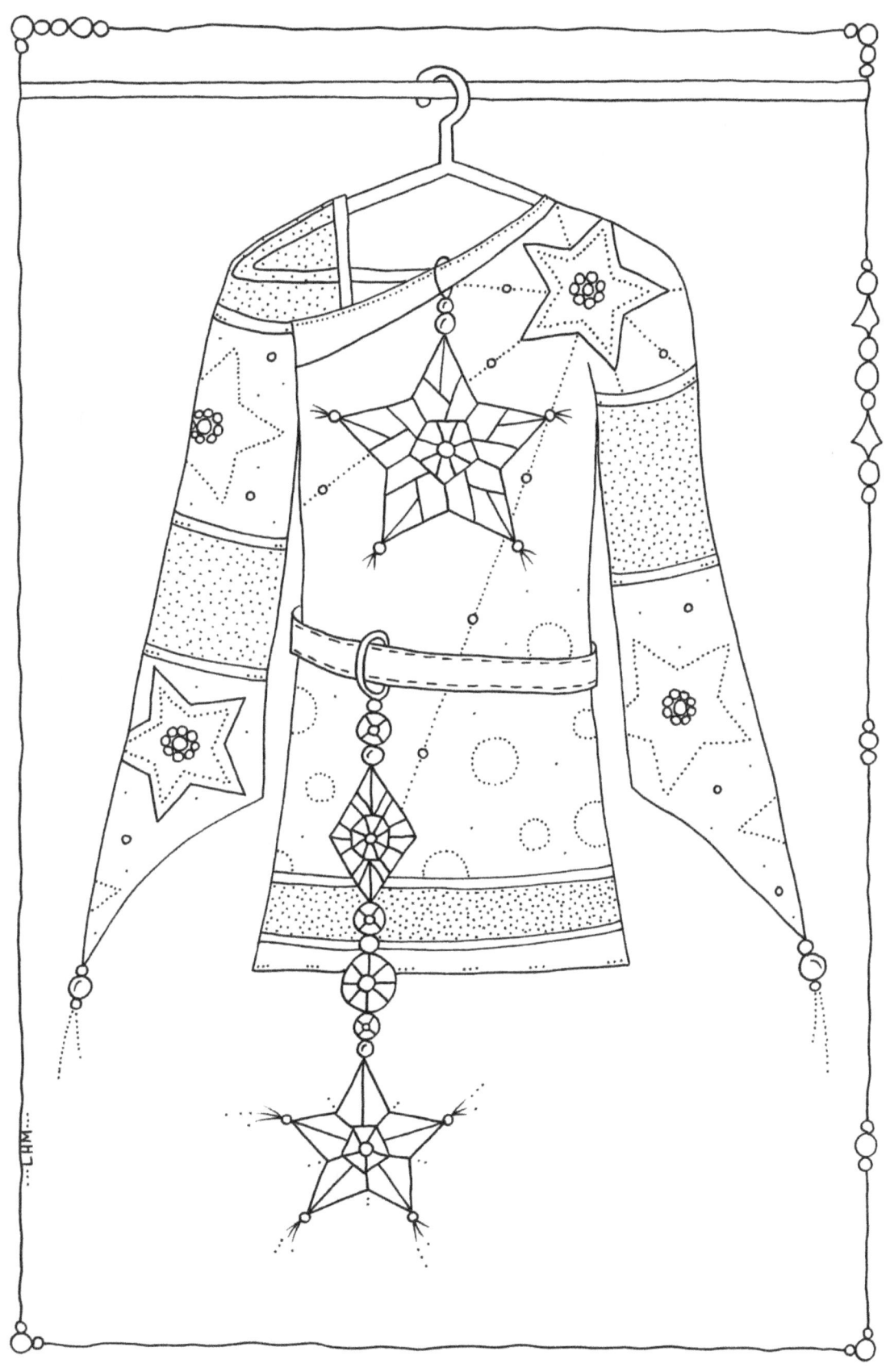

A5 - Postcard size images

The images in this section are all A5 - Postcard sized.

You have my permission to print them out as many times as you wish, for your own personal use.

They may not be used for commercial use without my prior written consent.

If you would like to make these into postcards, after coloring cut them out, and send them as a postcard, or large cards. If you print them directly onto thickish card you can send them as they are. If you print onto thin card, or paper (as I do), just mount them onto card with stick glue and a brayer, or double-sided tape after coloring.

You can then add embellishments. Glitter, washi tape, rubber stamping, 3D embellishments if you're feeling adventurous. Have fun, and experiment.

Then pop on a stamp and post!

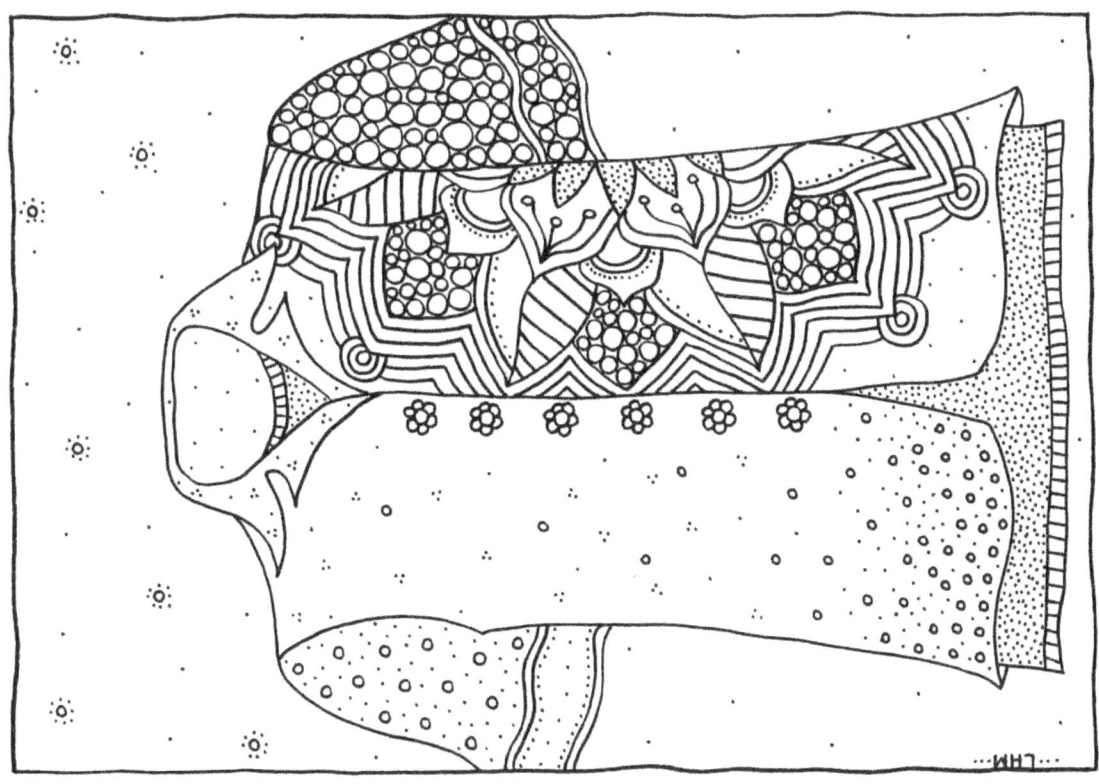

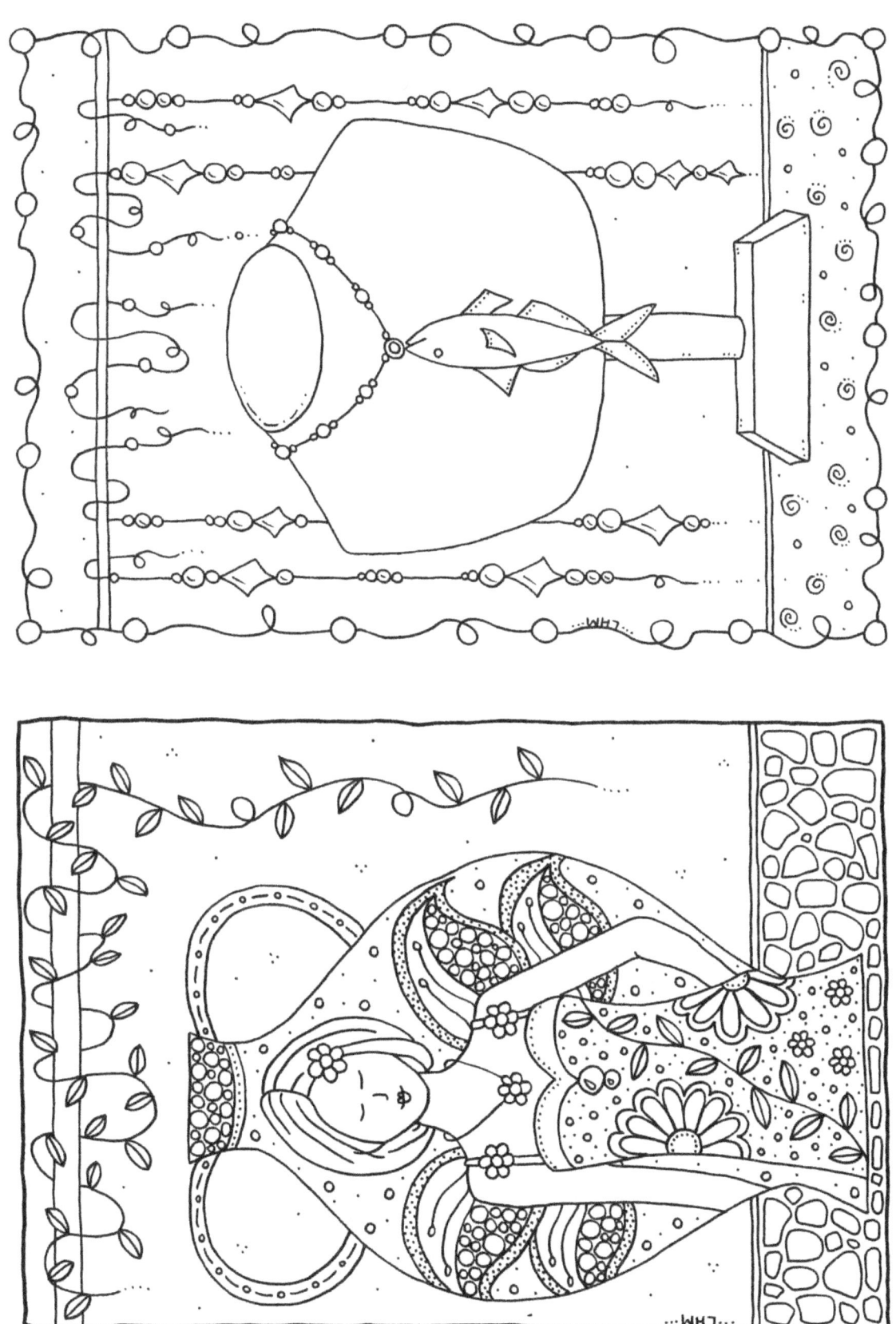

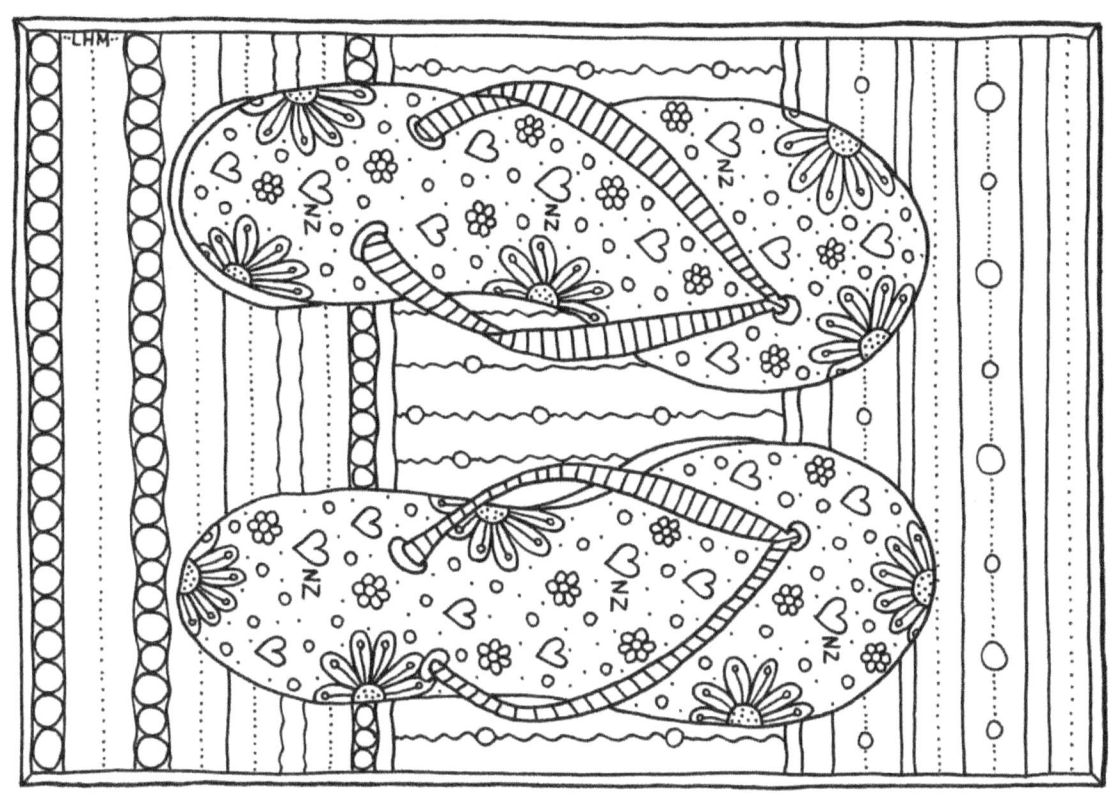
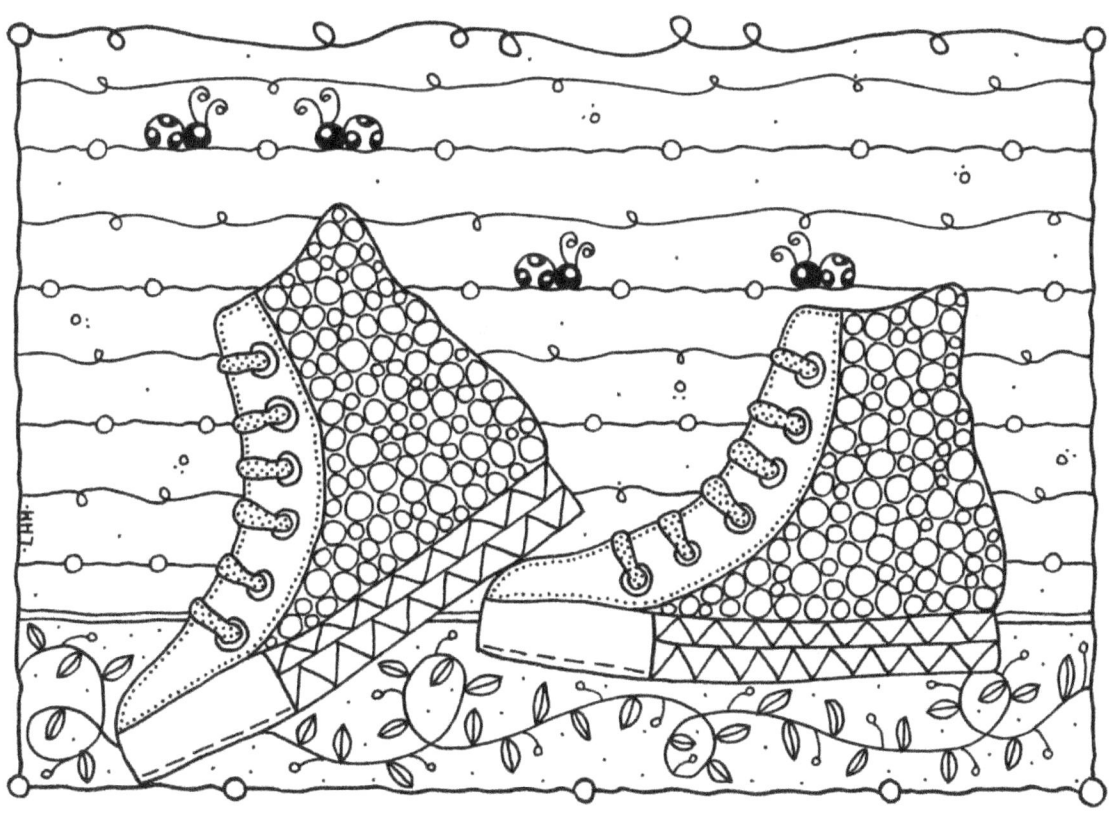

BONUS PAGES!

From my upcoming Mandala book.

I have only recently started drawing mandalas, and I'm slowly perfecting them. They're a lot more fun to draw than I originally thought, so yes, there WILL be a Wobbly Lines Mandala Book.

ENJOY!

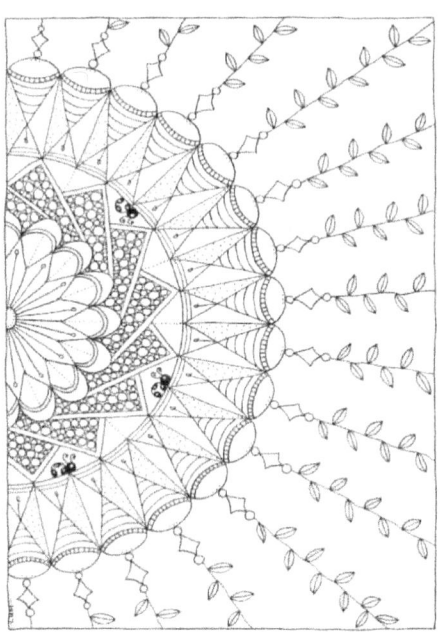

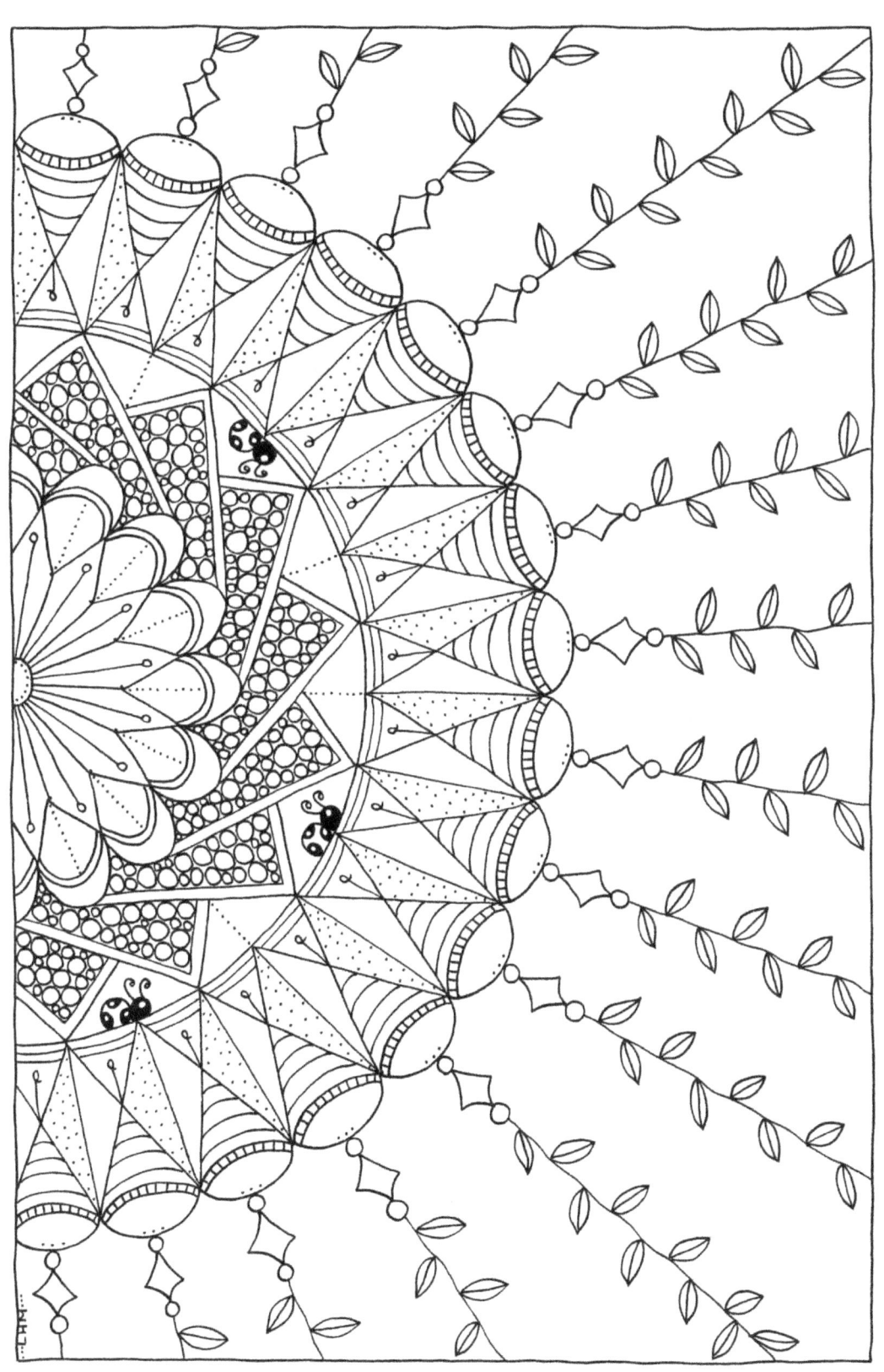

Acknowledgments:

There are so many people that I need to thank. Where do I begin?

My beloved cousin, Karen, for being one of my best friends, and for calling me Lindy Lou. Without you, I wouldn't be the person I am today, and this book would not have a name. x

My siblings.
My children.
My grandchildren.
My friends.
For loving me, supporting me, believing in me.

My parents, for always being there for me.

My daughters. My wonderful, amazing, gorgeous, loving, supportive daughters. Kylie-Mae and Dallas -   sweet, kind, generous, clever, artistic, fashionable ... did I leave anything out!?? LOL I love you both. xx

Shawn. Thank you, thank you, thank you! Your friendship, help and support has kept me going, I appreciate you more than you could imagine.

Finn, Joel & Layne. My boys. Thank you for choosing me to be your nan, and for the days we've spent together since you were all born, and for all the days we're going to have.   I love you to the moon and back. And to the zoo. And to the moon again. xxx

A thank you to all the wonderful people I've met since I started my art journey. To the colourers of my art, to the purchasers of my books, to my Patreon supporters, to all the amazing friends I've made. Thank you!

And my husband Greg. None of this would have been possible without you. You're my best friend, my love, my heart. Thank you for everything. xxxx